Valley Meditation (with Palomino)

poems by

PB Rippey

Finishing Line Press
Georgetown, Kentucky

Valley Meditation
(with Palomino)

ACKNOWLEDGMENTS

Askew Poetry Journal, "Run"

Chaparral, "Reseda Wind", "A Laugh"

The Pedestal Magazine, "Stranded"

anderbo.com, "The Sixth Appointment"

Publisher: Leah Maines

Editor: Christen Kincaid

Cover Art: Susan Bush

Author Photo: Scott Strohmaier

Cover Design: Elizabeth Maines

Printed in the USA on acid-free paper.
Order online: www.finishinglinepress.com
      also available on amazon.com

Author inquiries and mail orders:
Finishing Line Press
P. O. Box 1626
Georgetown, Kentucky 40324
U. S. A.

Table of Contents

For Scott and Taylor,
fellow Valley dwellers.
And for my sisters.

Bright Spot Through Wires

I pointed out Griffith Observatory.
He said: through those wires?
I said: Yes. He nodded
as if he had no qualms
with my particular mangy view
of heterogeneous city. I think,
in fact, he was preoccupied,
having left prescription glasses
inside, high on my kitchen counter
with the rest of his emptied pockets—
metal-ish mannish items: clipped
bills, a pocket knife. Could he see
the bright dome of the observatory?
He saw the wires. On a clear day, I
pressed, you can see the Hollywood
sign. I wasn't looking at him, not directly,
but caught his nod—the type of slow
solo nod I might give mortality.
I liked it, but worried: I invited him
to my balcony of sky and scape
to watch the sun drop, this dusk
confined by haze like a sad sea
creature netted, hauled to a surface,
forced on display. One thought dug
into me like nails: *You can't see it.*
You can't see it. You can't...

Later, after pan-fried tilapia and red
potatoes, he confessed he was a dolphin
in another life. And in yet another, a sea
turtle. I was astonished. He struck me
as a man of logic like narrow ladders,

simple-cousin equations applied to office
and home (should he ever visit there), com-
pass brain clicking, green, chartable eyes.
Perhaps he was, in fact, a lunatic. I liked it.
And I had to know: How did you die?

1.   shredded by sharks drunk on the blood of sea lions—
      too close, reckless, too
      close.

2.   a simple drift to the bottom of a fathom,
      an acute sense of 100 years
      following like a pleasant
      fluttering
      shroud.

I liked it. Slasher death. Gentle death.
I sipped my yellow wine, I laughed out loud
just as the green eyes slipped
from mine

and I was lost.

Midnight, city light wriggly as live bait,
the kiss a mild struggle reeking of déjà vu
and off he went. This is what happened next:

On the balcony—nursing a burn, dis-
secting the kiss—I watched his headlights
coast and bob down the one-way street
I live on, a dusky rise named for canyon
echoes and echoing mayhem down there
(invite someone new into that). The distant
howl of a famished coyote became brakes
whining, then screaming. Reverberation

whumped the far canyon wall, then my
wall: a city slit of instant war. I closed
my eyes, tuned in: *What Happened.*
Get The Hell Off Me. Then, nothing.
No sirens. No helicopter swinging
a rousting beam. I thought:

> *This is all new. You don't know—*
> *how could you when I ask questions*
> *in the middle of a surefire kiss, but I*
> *had a title I died for. Too close. So*
> *reckless! Get off me...What*
> *happened. Nothing. Except that I*
> *died. I did. I*
> *died.*

He left in time
(green eyes slipping).

Oh, yes:
he also died a soldier's death in WWII. Shot in the head.
He's not saying it's real. Not one of his *lives,*
lives. But he's open: what can't be proven
might be true?

I like it. How can I
not.

Run

Sun the fog's ball snagged by a suburban barrier
of giraffe-necked palms. My lawn in recess: churched
        (this formal stillness, fog-tuned).
My lawn is Winter's readied bride, her chill-
wrap tight over tips, her delicate sweat.
        Here, the deciduous
whisper off leaves by evening's folding light
as I watch 2 boys chasing impulse

in cold separating fog framing the moon risen
so early in her hypocrisy of flaws
        (O pocked resilience).
Run, run.
Their rocket gasps, blood-worked
        tidal energy
pushed the length of my yard's walls
of safe as I summon a time-traveling

domesticity and grippable martyrs:
books I resented others owning
        until I arrived
in this pocket of breathy Eden,
clueless. Cold frills the air. I watch:
        the moon bent on counter-
clockwise logic, her pale eye's glass-cuts
old trickery I won't translate. Won't.

Run. Run.
Sun shatters into anemone sky.
        My speck-titans so suddenly famous:
they in their sweet hides, I in my cloak-bane,
howling
        with half-sight, knocked (*I get: you!*),
                ever on the chase.

Valley Meditation (with Palomino)

You are either with me, or against me.
—Harrison Gray Otis

Acquiring Otis christened a town: Marian,
after his daughter. Widower Chandler chose
Marian for his bride (or Otis chose her
for him). Marian became: Mrs. Marian
Otis Chandler—and widower Chandler? #1
in Otis' megalopolis of Los Angeles rag.
Later, Marian downgraded into a fragrant,
non-native plant: Reseda, but the woman's
maiden name slid-to, intact. She kept it
(or, Otis had her keep it for him). *You,
why you are either with me or against me.*
O powers that be.

Google Reseda: corner pawn shop, span-
ning false front straight out of Maverick
(Diamonds! Watches! Guns!), main
attraction in city a pocket watch smashed.
I prefer the 3rd and final floor of that Macy's:
tinted window rivaling a mogul's personal
movie screen: sky a blue scream exhaling
thunderheads, strap-flat suburbia smog-
ringed, as though atom bomb lifts yet
from valley floor—world mirage-robbed,
grossly underdreamt. Streetside: tobacco
kiosks, little barred fortresses, per-
sisting.

Melvin. Shirley. Wilbur. Louise. I have
yet to find Marian Rd., though Otis thrives
down the block and, spanning suburbia's
blunt ends: *Chandler, Chandler, Chandler.*
Louise. Wilbur. Shirley. Melvin. Did Marian
know them? Swap cobbler recipes, tips
for grilling barracuda fished from Catalina's

aquarium-ocean? Did she sail the varnished
schooners tipping men in suspenders, their shirt-
sleeves rolled to snowy shoulders? In petticoat
and ironed pinafore, did she haul in the catch side
by side with her mate? Shuck corn, gossip in
this sun-like-a-star's-death-reaching-us? Pipe
smoke, unmarked beer bottles the deep amber
of thirst, graffiti vining our alley's cinderblock,
gun-runs tobacco kiosk to kiosk, some
particularly rough-pink twilights hinging
on the organic martini as wind thwacks
a neighbor's roof with a wrenched power
line, our portion of valley exed out, our per-
sonal patch: crater, cradle, footprint, rain-
less—here, our neighbors are (thank you!)
nameless.

Louise is my stepfather's elegant mother
languishing between memory and sleep
in the seaside town I ache for daily.
I have never known a Wilbur I could like.
Shirley is a movie star, dwindled/dead.
Melvin? His ripped chainlink frames
a kid's school, mustard-colored huts
shelter from the type of wild heat
Melvin sought to wield, razing orange
groves in his bit of frenzy, against
nothing, opportunist, child's prank! Gut-
ting.

In Sunday's heat-knit dusk
I glance up from pinching pie crust
into old-fashioned, part curtains
patterned in stem-joined cherries.

A golden palomino trots my street,
her rider guiding with the blythe
sway of a professional. *Hup, Marian!*
The rocking canter. By the time I yell
for the world and stumble outside, man
and horse are a yellow star, a juicy
glistening on the wane, clopping
echoing into epic, towards Chatsworth's
deformed cliffs red as fire in the sun's
dregs, seared boulder chop: a madwoman's
teeth, baring. On,
on.

Otis also named a freighter after Marian,
ton after ton of her slinking into harbor
Chandler founds. The freighter, too,
rechristened: Empire Leonard, put
to war for you and you. O foolish
crossings. The sinking of 5,767
tons.

O tall handsome girl, major stock-
holder donning pearls/aprons, worker-
bee, working mother to 8. With them,
against them (the shocking burials,
Boomtown's ugly molts) you kept
your odd post. Steady. Name(s)
intact.

Reseda Wind

Our neighbor (a stranger, we are new
here, fresh from another hard-ocher valley
more

risky/cosmopolitan, though as baldly sunned)
warned us wind is rare summers.
Obviously

she is never homebound weekdays, 3-ish,
when (as if brewed in a pot of heat/
hide,

swung loose by an iron arm) wind arrives,
ripping dried fronds from palms like skirts
from

unsuspecting spinsters forever pathetically
standing by; leaf-looting shenanigans be-
heading

non-native plants, snapping ribs
of my shade umbrella; wolf's breath, hurting
specific

treasures cherished earlier, when my child and I
played so well. Chimes panic, dead-drop
from

the orange tree outside his modest bedroom's window;
my hair stolen from the silver clip; ox shoulders
clumsy

my watering of scorched bush and weed and I wonder:
where have we moved now, 13 miles closer to my sea
though

barely inching across basin scavenged by trespassing
poets (tattlers, thieves); odds-off country; even the potato
vine's

raveled locks parted—the new grave's rock
headstone sheeny in our soldier-sun, reminder of the one
senseless

casualty of this change (*O sacrifice, you who never knew,* etc.).
And when it's finished its donkey's yawn over my yard, wind
reaches

for an outrage of thunderheads, rolling them peak-white
over sky pressed into a tryst with obscurity—one
un-

mined poetic scream summing up the rest
of this year's ordinary calamities—
wind

vanishing, returning, breathing heat-shiny gems
I am stupid to dismiss: a child's treasures, a death,
chimes,

my
own silently spun headlines petri-
fying
in mid-summer's heave.

If The World Really Looks Like That

If the world really looks like that I will paint no more.
—Claude Monet

Trees sprouting from within trees—
mad bloom in the bloom—

brash fertility.
If I scrutinize

the chronic melt of loomed mountains
long enough, I will go blind. Tell

me: will you die here?
Or (flat hat in hand) create.

Alone in groggy afternoon
your heart is a quake in murky heat,

your city's heel askew on shying pebbles:
beauty alone won't support the poet

as well-ransacked poets know,
here, watching you un-

earth bodies in mute, flagrant
paradise.

When I ask, Paradise?
My house, you say. Again—

will you die
or summon another stroke—

such admired strokes *(heat, bella,*
heat). You are the wedding

yucca, wildly in season—
your blossom-white shudders,

muddled poise. You are the villa's
one-shadow, dim re-

life in mobbing foliage. You. Maniac—
your racy impressions, obstinate fire

bushes, persistent, overripe mauves:
Wander on. I seek

some guide of my own, one
strictly paradise-rapt,

her hand over mine
as we meet quavering distance,

the continental villa-calm—
anything but motionless peopling

your Master Street. If the world
really looks like that? Clarity
before I'm done.

Stranded

You choose a foot, a head and a vertebra
(you think) sunblasted skin-smooth, tugged
from seawall rising above island beach
like an ambitious art installation: wall
of contemporary junk fused by sea
in all her panoramic moods, ferried
by swell, squalls here, where you
and I are the last two on earth. Naked
but for hiking boots and sunglasses
we excavate green bottles, flip-flops, life
vests, surfboards halved, one whole
anchor, a car's fender (confetti-rust),
a rubber duck trapped in a mold packed
by deft, transparent fingers and although
nothing is unfamiliar. we are shocked
to find it here, like Warhol shocks us
into viewing the mundane as a personal
flaw—mine, yours. Boy-romantic, you choose
the organic: pig skull, atrophied bird's foot,
mystery vertebra weighed in your hands—
bright, appalling fragment. Dusk mottles
the shallows and the first shark fin
of the evening glides by two feet
from my boots. Land, you shout,
pointing to California—a spine brown
as the air blurring scarred peaks. A-
round us, life clings to rocks—limpets,
glossed mussels, seals. Pelicans stab
the swell. Gull wings flare above pitted
cliffs. There is no escaping it, you say, fit-
ting skull, foot and vertebra into
your khaki sack—a perfect
fit.

I can't take my eyes off the sharks.

Gull

The Book a pamphlet. Stapled
spine and brief. Pen and ink
illustrations of puzzled faces,
the victims, I supposed, struggling
to grip their receding souls. Text
meant to crush surprise, but surprise
was all we had left of him—breath-deep:
in, out, stop—in, out...
Surprise.

The Pamphlet was a map, from X,
to X. I*neffectual, wrong*, I lobbied,
but my sisters had to read and so I
did, too. Four of us, united, at least.
The nurse praised our tending,
our bond (nurtured from dust into
a frayed banner since his brief,
vicious reign—our clever escapes,
cinematic touchdowns, decades-
spun reboots). Thank you, we told
his nurse, but, really: how dare
she.

The Map led us through where we'd been,
explained *why* like a TV sort the weather,
why he flicked the hem of his cotton sheet
with a forefinger as though ridding it
of nibs (check), dementia (check);
the perverse coma, its bucking chest,
its still-life chest w/fish gasps, fixed
belaboring of life. We soldiered on:
the soul has flown! Despite the baby-
pulse—*Stormed off, actually*, I thought,

irked by the cheaply bound passed
hands to hands over rail-framed bed
deep in a stifling seaside condo
I've visited half my life. *Oh*, this!
we agreed, tapping a page when gasps
rattled. *Yes. This*. We waited. Looked
away. Read.

Outside, a turquoise birdbath on the tiny
patio, its water light in September's im-
pertinent heat and finch-less and raven-less.
In sky, a gull body-straddled wind ex-
haled from Baja's decrepit jut, pewter
wings instinctually adjusting their
nod.

Middlings

We are the middle mothers—joy-
ful some muse-sifted afternoons,
those, frankly, slept through, dreamless.
We are hovering neo-classics hunting
for lawns vast enough for our fallen
rainbow parachutes, mouse-wheels,
muddled antics of sacred feet.
We tend our wrist watches dawn
to noon to twilight, marking the skies
for simple signs we share wordlessly,
each to her owned, each owned similarly
dealt, though discussion exposes mixed
wiring. Mostly, we are misunderstood,
a baying herd of grief-wary Cassandras
rounding up strays, thinning peril
with our breasts until darkness
vanquishes us home to our mad
Trucevilles-kitchens: dishing,
spooning, meddling
it right.

The Sixth Appointment

On the sixth appointment (your
third) I rattled off the plot
of *Washington Square*, your hand
circling my knee, your reach strained
(I don't know why we didn't simply
scoot you close), city sun lightening lab-
yellow blinds and when I couldn't look
at you I spoke to the naked baby squatting
in a porcelain bowl on the wall—its squidge,
its stupid smile, hair sparse as an old man's
(when we were shown in, we laughed
at the sight of him) and when I couldn't
look at the baby I gazed at the replica
of certain anatomy (purple plastic
for the womb, gum-red for the cervix,
pink for It, etc.), a piece you joked
lonely bachelors might display
in their bedrooms and when I spoke
to you again the sun had your eyes,
hoarding their godly-green and the room
spun and I sat back and you rose as the doctor
entered in stylish platform sandals, pleasant
skirt beneath the coat and the two of you
shared a laugh before she whipped open
her magic chart, divined the unseen, lifted
my new blouse, squirted on the goop, pressed
the thing home and you heard (for the first time)
the tiny, persistent galloping. And nobody
laughed, then, except me, because I'd for-
gotten (*even after all these fucking visits*):
miracles breathe.

A Laugh

Today: I wander on hands
and knees—weary, visual
sweep in a den of primary
colors and day-old loot ro-
tated with yesterday's loot
mixed with gifts shelved
months ago, while he mut-
ters to a TV screen, dis-
tracted.

A grey grain of cat litter. A-
nother. Beneath the piano's eerie
claw-legged arc, blackened fruit
peel, a stray unpopped corn kernel
shiny as a watered pearl. Outside,
the lot with its crawl of machines
and men, dust veiling rattled
windows framing a yellow crane
lumbering on: sad beast, savage
sucked out of it. In my quick
private silence: Dvorak,

always his No. 9,
No. 9, No. 9. That day?
O my fine drugged hours,
swirly room, suns burst-
ing locked centers, peace
reigning in a drip, in a drip in-
to me as he slumbered or stared.
Together we were stunning
by dark or day, tight in a bond
of fresh deeds; envied. I pocket
the litter grain, kernel, the lot
nattering on: tremors, another

beast passing, wetted dirt
cramming slow jaws.
He is riveted by the ADD

puppet on the screen. Look:
miniature gaze of a minute
man processing an actor's lines—
not one year shelved since those
friends I loved quailed from the
3D O of belly, from miracle-
workings, unable to express why
in language other than im-
penetrable as I rocked him,
as I rock him into day, into night
in this shook hole (shock-
hole), consistently saving a life.
The puppet laughs, red as a devil,
jittery-bold giggles testing jump-
ing minds of those gone rock-
ing to sway, rock, sway.
Today: O my tiny poverty!
O secret strain!

Waste

I heard your story: her dead ex-husband, coffin lid
slung wide; her loose sermon (slurred, muddled-heretic)
tongues)…

I saw you: chauffeur to her un-
fortunate son transfixed
by

a blipping game-eats-
game. As she played docent
for

a minor throng, you escorted that boy
in. I heard you: shifting my elbows on
table

in a salt-bitten Sunday outdoors—a creep
of fresh fog over the Queen Mary's
slanted

black stacks, there, across drowsing harbor,
parents waiting on children
dawdling

before laminated
podiums ex-
plaining

where waste goes—*There*, a boy told us when, earlier,
we strolled, touching—bold, tiny stranger with sunny
curls

and big-boy sandals—*There*, he raged, indicating harbor
water, his people explaining: *he knows too much* but he was 4,
or

40, Christ, how could *I* know? You saw me. I pointed
to the fog, whispered *incoming.*
Who

is watching? you ask as a child dares
tender heels upon a chair at the troubled table
near

ours, howls, wobbles so that we… Our baby (should
we) we declared earlier (strolling, touching),
will

receive a sturdy name. You said:
John-James, Block, Gunter.
I

said: *Crumpling, Strewner, Rip?* Who is there?
you repeat. Parents tend menus. Stacks
sleep.

Listen: her son glimpsed Hell in church—returned
to the blips. Cheap escape? Possibly. But even
screens

sift. Even older, what we grow into! Children,
children everywhere. Testing. Raging.
Oh

you with the dark coat
draping your arm,
your

green eyes burning
when she made her son
look—

well, they don't love you, but I will,
I do, this deep into Sunday, salvaging my
crew.

Doomsday

Inherited clay pot slit by shade-roots
I imprisoned with felt hums; corn plant's
bent stalk's permanent struggle; geraniums

thriving—perverse creatures the cheap pink
of cocktail parasols, adapting. House finches

nest in the arc of an electricity meter high
on the wall of the plaster building opposite.

Next month: they will erase the structure.
What of the birds? Or trees in front—old heat

lovers shedding musk and orange hippie blossoms?
What of the feral cats dug in deep beneath foundation,

cool in their won maze, unloved, alive? Loved, I hang
a fibrous shade from eaves, blocking a rise of appalling

values. This deep into city-thought, the end
of the world is a way of life. We are meek hostages

of heat, the sour air. *Heat kills.* The cats breeding
in their shade-drawn watch know it. Who am I

to bring the squalling into this? Each grid glows
with sun-warp, stripped to cement, even the river re-

laid on her poured bed, her castle-banks bird-less.
Some dawns? A whiff: coastcall cool as a swindler's

jazzy blue sleeve. Our street? Gulls wail the world
from lampposts instead of masts. Night from Mulholland's

dipping spine: valley lit ocean mouthing a dry red. There!
My foot is drenched. Run-off streaks months of built dust.
Listen: inside, he presses the vital button this soon. The air
conditioner's blow-box booms.

Full Flower Moon

May (mostly), the petticoat swirl
of opening meadow, pinkening bud.
I say: rose, peony, phlox. And I say: petal-
shorn, plucked, blown until only the head
remains, one pale sticky oval crushed by u-
niverse so formidable it upgrades the dead
into blossoming. Old flower-face—you!
Cruel palette-eye! Where, where is your color?
I say: dearest, warmest, sugar-phlox fairy.
Dare I say: more. It's May (mostly). And I
am showered and sweet beneath puckered
moonlight, stem right behind an ear. I am thigh-
deep in meadow and I must know: are you
dressed? Staunch, seasonal gloom cut? Dancy,
gleamy blue-fires broken through? Show
me. The moon requires it. I confess: May.
More! I confess the kiss: a peony, phlox,
a peony, phlox, a peony, phlox, the
rose.

PB Rippey's work has appeared in many journals, including *Zyzzyva, Chaparral, Askew Poetry Journal, The Pedestal Magazine Phoebe, Slope, Pool, Runes, Solo, anderbo.com, Poetry NZ* and *Other Voices International*. She is the recipient of the 2007 Abroad Writers' Conferences Poetry Fellowship and has been a Finalist in contests ranging from *Glimmer Train* to the *Rona Jaffe Writers' Awards*. She is the author of the poetry chapbook, *Nightmares with Moons* (Pudding House Press). A seventh generation Californian, she lives in the vast, heat-layered West San Fernando Valley with her husband and second grader and mini-zoo of rescued animals.

www.ingramcontent.com/pod-product-compliance
Lightning Source LLC
LaVergne TN
LVHW091236080426
835509LV00009B/1311